Equanimity

Equanimity

Poems by

Ed Ryterband Ph.D.

© 2025 Ed Ryterband. All rights reserved.
This material may not be reproduced in any form, published,
reprinted, recorded, performed, broadcast,
rewritten, or redistributed without
the explicit permission of Ed Ryterband.
All such actions are strictly prohibited by law.

Cover design by Shay Culligan
Cover image by Ed Ryterband
Author photo by Ed Ryterband

ISBN: 978-1-63980-899-1

Kelsay Books
502 South 1040 East, A-119
American Fork, Utah 84003
Kelsaybooks.com

I dedicate this volume to my wife, Madelyne, and our sons, Jason and Michael, who continue to encourage this special endeavor. I tip my hat to fellow poets at US1 Poetry Cooperative who make life worthy of capturing on the page.

Finally, there are the nourishing memories of Sondra Gash, who became a special friend and Nancy Scott, who, along with Sondra, was a poet and teacher, whose patient wisdom woke me up to the possibilities of poetry and the rigors of developing this craft.

Acknowledgments

Thank you to the following publications, in which versions of these poems previously appeared:

Publications (Noted by an*):
The Comic Strip: "Wanting to be Dangerous"
Paterson Literary Review: "Homecoming," "Big Boys"
Two River Times: "Off to College," "November Memories"
US 1 Worksheets: "Night Cruller, " "Inside Jokes," "The Troubadour," "Flowered Tumblers," "The Looks of Love," "Mother's Gone"

Readings:
The Atrium in Red Bank
Brookdale Community College
The Enclave in Shrewsbury
The New Bruinswick Public Library
The Oceanside Library
Parkside Lounge in NYC

Readings disguised as standup comedy performances in NYC:
Catch a Rising Star
The Comic Strip
Mostly Magic
The Piano Bar

Contents

About "Equanimity"

PROLOGUE

Meditating on Equanimity   17

FAMILY

40 Years and Counting	21
Night Cruller	22
Remember Love on a Winter Day	23
Message to Her Grownup Sons	24
Big Boys	25
Off to College	26
Homecoming	28
Bathtub Captain	30
Kitchen Blues	32
Deep Night Journey	34

IN THE WORLD

Another Autumn	39
Goldfish	40
Inside Jokes	42
iPhone Upgrade	43
November Memories	45
Our Seasons	46
The Encyclopedia Britannica	47
The Guitar Player in the Square	48
The Troubadour	51
Beige	52

WISHES

Facebook Post from the Buddha	55
First Girlfriend	57
Flowered Tumblers 1953	58
Wanting to Be Dangerous 1955	60
What's Your Favorite Food?	62
Ode to Coney Island	63
Set Fire to the Rain	64
The Looks of Love	65
Loved One Nostalgia	66
Spring Morning on the Back Porch	67
When I Leave Up the Toilet Seat	68

OLD AGE

Still Working After All These Years	71
Reflections on a Winter Evening	73
Elder Morning	75
Mother's Gone	77
The Wheelchair in the Den	78
Their Suitcase in the Basement	79
August Surrender	82
The Physics of Time and Me	84
My Plan for Becoming Dead	85
Resolutions	86

About "Equanimity"

Things are just as they are. All things are impermanent. Joy and sorrow arise and pass away. I am safe in this moment. These meditation phrases have nourished me in my later years. This volume is about how I got to that place and sometimes didn't. These are reflections that have become prominent in my 80s; about the people in my whole life, the world around me, the political and religious beliefs driving that world which I can't ignore; the wishes that drive me now; the stark fact of aging.

PROLOGUE

Meditating on Equanimity

I meditate so I won't
ruminate about the past
pinched again
by sharp fingers of regrets
hurts inflicted, paths not followed.

I meditate so I won't
agitate about the future
driven and depleted
do I have enough
do I do enough.

I meditate so I will
rest in this moment
things are just as they are
joy and sorrow arise and pass away
all things are impermanent
including me.

Surrender is a tricky skill.

FAMILY

40 Years and Counting

I want you very much to love me.
Who is better
my tenured partner
to nudge me to my next appointments.

You are audience and leading lady
featured in my fables
stories I bring to life
burnished conquests and rebellions.

Time pokes me with its wicked finger.
You help me hold my ground
sometimes stare it down
distract me when I need it.

Your comforts help me
embrace my soft illusions.
moments where I forget
I'm in a life that ends without you

a time I give infrequent notice
yet it will surely come
foist itself upon me
like a cat upon an unsuspecting mouse.

Night Cruller*

In their bedroom he and she
lay down in their chosen sides
drop off into sleep

begin their wheezes, cover tussles
snorts begetting mid-sleep interruptions
when he'd lurch out for the bathroom

in the trance learned long ago
ending when he'd slip
politely back into his half

except this night
he lifts the cover slow and careful
creeps across the great divide

feels her, bites her shoulder
soothes it with his lips
wiggles close until, voila, she wiggles back.

Without a word
they twist their bodies into one
this giant cruller . . .

He whispers close into her ear
You are my food, my just dessert.

He smiles to himself
she must be smiling too.

Remember Love on a Winter Day

We do have our melody
despite the noise

doubts I tangle with
sharp edges of regrets

tomorrows I try to never think of
insist themselves on me.

I do hear our love tune
interrupted and renewed.

I remember you do love me
in your certain way.

There's nothing left to prove
just see you, be here and relent.

When you went into your sleep
I watched you.

My breathing eased.
My pulse went slower, slower.

My focus narrowed
finally to feel the moment

in this fragile place in me that loves.

Message to Her Grownup Sons

I know you care for me
and judge me.
I suspect your whispers
We love her, but . . .

You have so much else to occupy you
but when you've left
your being young
sooner than you guess

umbilicus long shriveled
you'll also be less visible
someone people sometimes visit
after all, it is the thing to do.

Still I wish
from time to time
you'd put aside what else
who else there is

come and stay
listen to my stories
maybe you'll discover once again
the warm of me around you.

Big Boys*

They're coming home for the weekend.
40 and 34, agile, strong and fatless.
They used to crowd the doorway.
Now I wait behind the door for them.
They are grown forever.

I've read to them in bed
saw them off to camp, to college,
watched them emigrate to other lives.
I loved them more than I expected.
Time is a wicked shadow.

I get the door before they ring the bell.
Come on in; put your stuff down.
How are things Dad?
I feel like I did 30 years ago.
Together: *The problem is I still can count.*

I should make sure they know.
I hold railings on the stairs.
I miss more things that people say.
My hand shakes when I eat my soup.
Have they already noticed?

Off to College*

I see you standing close
curly hair, lean and quick.
We don't look each other in the eye.

Every picture conjures
a vapor trail
leads back to where I've sealed you.

Steering your stroller
humming to you
in an early morning's empty streets.

Sitting on your bed
your eyes sweet and endless
begging for a story

scary, just enough
a tale of pirates, Inca treasures
hermit's ghosts.

I feel a swallow
inside jaws clenched tight,
tin whistling in my ears.

I stare down to the floor
eyelids squinting
like staring into sunlight.

A long inhale rescues me.
The sob I wrestle with recedes.
Sorrows mix with benedictions for your future.

Tonight we talked about you
the joys, good wishes
we lavished on you.
Your mom
her lips squeezed out
she tried to stop . . .

I want him to come back.
I'll put him on the carpet
and just stare at him.

You're gone
except in noiseless flashes
attic memories.

Homecoming*

Your welcome hug long
enough to say you really missed us.
Stubble-faced wiry man child
in our home again.

It's still your room
your polar bear
resting on your pillow
white fur a little yellowed.

We all eat together.
You and I play man-boy games
punching, wrestling.
You're quicker, stronger now.

I tell myself
I'm more clever
and relentless.
I still can win.

Afterwards I urge
myself to ask you
an upbeat, friendly query.
So, what's new?

I hope you'll shrink my worries.
You mutter, bob and weave
offer only shadows.
I cannot shine a light inside.

I almost try again, relent instead
give up my routines
clean up in your wake
love you without hope
smile when you leave.

Bathtub Captain

His days begin
checking down inside his pj's
for first arrival pubic hairs.
His twelve-year-old obsessions
flit from how he'll do at bat
to girls imagined naked.

This fateful evening in the tub
The Captain spies a U-Boat
coming close
a slowly growing target.
From the hall his mother barks
When are you coming out?

Soon.
The Captain presses on.
Up periscope.
He waits until the moment comes.
His very first torpedo.
He lets it go . . . a hit.

The Captain stops
stares down in the tub.
So are you coming out?

He's jolted, breathes again
leaps out, dries his body off
jumps into his navy-blue pajamas.

Behind the door
he's still bewildered, frightened
is his body broken?

Kitchen Blues

I'm 6, he's 9.
It's dinner time
we play with food
not serious.
He flicks a pea at me.
I plot revenge
load up two beauties on my fork.

Suddenly our father's eyes squeeze shut
hairy hands choke the table edge.
Goddammits spew between his gritted teeth
his fist attacks
our redwood kitchen table
his dish flies up
flips upside down and crashes.

He bolts off down the hall
slams shut the bathroom door.
The blast noise splits my ears.
My body jumps up straight.
Behind the door, sharp clatter.
A tile's flown out from the wall
shatters on the bathroom floor.

A slick of fear roils in my skinny gut.
Time to stare at food
clasp our hands.
Minutes crawl.
He comes back to the kitchen
takes his place
a looming silence.

Next day I blurt out to our mother
let's run away together
find a place for just us three.
A long moment stands between us.
She looks straight at me.
Then, her steady, even words
Your father is a good provider.
Go outside and play.

Deep Night Journey

I trundle to the bathroom
along my familiar path.
Before another round of sleep
I follow signs of night life in our bedroom.

Pale green glows from the alarm clock.
Smoke detector twinkles on the ceiling.
Moonlight stripes tiptoe through the shutters
on their silent passage to our bedroom wall.

My notice
flows outside the window
follows scattered sounds
night world invitations.

A commuter train
its hoarse laments
announce across the dark
its muscular assurance to deliver
weary strangers to their parking lots.

A truck
its grinding gear shifts
whining higher, higher
calling out its slog
along a late night highway.

The wind
breathing through our naked winter trees
rises, urges me to listen.
I track its slow fall into silence
returning me into our night inside.

I allow my journey's end
turn my body on its side
feel my eyes close
hear your breathing
through the soft throat of your slumber

drop down again into our sleep.

IN THE WORLD

Another Autumn

This summer seared the earth.
It could be the end of days.
Still we squabble over climate change
like barnyard chickens.
    Autumn shows up once again
    gold, brown and crimson leaves
    ornament our maples.

Election day at last arrives.
Candidates end their clamor.
The people whoop
or curse or yawn.
    Autumn shows up once again
    a leaf cloud wind-brushed off our maple branches
    swirls outside the bedroom window

We revel over Our Thanksgiving.
Close our minds to immigrants
suffer in the certainty
strangers come to take our portion.
    Autumn shows up once again
    delivering its shorter, colder days
    crispy air, geese honking overhead.

Goldfish

If you're a goldfish in a pond
a spread of flies floating
on the water up above you
is an omelet.

You swim up
open up your fish lips
swallow down a crunchy brunch.
Life is good. You do not fret

about your manners
gluten free, organic flies
food allergies that could
make you break out in a rash.

You swim around that pond
your residence.
You gulp down all the flies you need.
They are your stash.

If you live in someone's parlor
a fish bowl's even better.
You don't know from *fish bowl, parlor.*
Everything at home is fine.

You don't have a word for morning
but when daylight comes
a hand appears, a packet shakes
out floats a pour of flies like wine

every day a feast of flies and flakes
enough for you and all the other fish
you look up, pucker up
say your fish thanks.

Inside Jokes*

My friend Alan asks me
did you hear the one about?...

I'm always on the lookout
for little pleasures
trust his offer
suspend my need to doubt
hope for a surprise

allow his story in about
Three people in a lifeboat
A horse walks into a bar
How fat was she . . .
then his punch line hits
a sudden twist

again I'm fooled.

The light pops in my ear
careens down to my belly.
My breath jumps out.
I'm unaware of time or anything,
just my laugh

like having sex
but friendlier, less messy.

iPhone Upgrade

The door says *OPEN*.
I obey, push through.
Late afternoon.
Few customers.

Those youngsters at their stations
look up from their cellphones
waiting for a chance
to serve

to sell, to snow me
with their foreign tongue
*iCloud Backup, pixels, software
password keychains . . .*

I'm on my feeble guard
one kid sidles up
*Welcome to Verizon. How can I help?
You're looking for a new phone? Perfect.*

*Do you have a trade in?
Thanks, I see it's been a while
You'll be surprised how much is new
and better for you.*

*Thus begins the blizzard
iCloud Backup, password keychains . . . ,*
I turn into a bobble head.
At last he stops to breathe.

Two hours, maybe three sneak by.
Once again I push the door
walk out into the parking lot
stop and stare at my iPhone upgrade.

November Memories*

A midday autumn sun
highlights brown and pointy oak leaves
dropping down at last on naked bushes.
Tufts of knee-high golden grasses shush beneath the breeze
a hillside stream gives subtle notice of its journey.

Edging down the grassy bank
I greet the sky lights flickering across the stream
crouch down at its edge, watch its rippled silver skin
trace eager fingers through the water's cool
inhale the succulence of rotting leaves.

I rise, walk slowly down the hillside
frame some pictures in my mind
to save these special moments
transform the stream, the hillside
into memories I'll hold and burnish over time.

Outside my flow of thoughts
the stream keeps gliding over stones
where in some distant era may succumb

roll unnoticed over little ledges
into quiet pools

or keep on
rolling down the hillside

into an endless sea somewhere.

Our Seasons

Cocooned inside forever nights
we try to put off waking
give in at last to fragile dawn lights
inching onto icy blue horizons.

Beyond the old front door
we just had painted red
April rains wash down
on our patient oaks and maples.

Day heat vapors rise up
into leaf filled branches
twilight lingers, invites us
to a sky top dusted end to end with stars.

Gilt and ochre leaf clouds
shimmer through our windowpanes
drift down and settle
on our newly frosted, acorn dotted lawn.

The Encyclopedia Britannica

Travels of a 12-year-old

This rainy Friday afternoon
I hug our brand-new set of fat blue books
juicy like an endless hotdog.

Aardvark all the way to Zygote
24 thick volumes
plus the Year Book 1952.

I open up the first book
sit legs crossed
flying on our living room beige carpet.

I dive into the colored map of Africa
say out loud unheard-of countries' names
imagine blazing sunsets on a place called Serengeti.

Later on I'll ride an elephant across the British Raj
fly with puffins over Coral Atolls
swim through rolling waves with Dolphins.

But then my travels have to pause.
I'm called home from Tanganyika
for lamb chops at our redwood kitchen table.

The Guitar Player in the Square

We leave our homes
swept along in airport throngs.
We fly at last away

until we're welcomed
back to solid earth
somewhere else.

We surrender to
our Guides with Colored Flags
who introduce themselves in smiles

and pack us in their van
to transport us to
Your Boutique Hotel.

We fall into the sleep we lost
taking us to sunrise
and the promises of pampering.

We recognize the toast and eggs
amid each table's
breakfast flower color riot.

The first day van ride
takes us to a summer vineyard
For a Health Hike

down a dirt and gravel path
alive with grape vines, flying bugs,
after-rain aromas.

Further on the path
we pass into
and through a gated village wall

that once would guard the peace
inside this hillside Spanish town
now alive with tourist gift shops.

Take some time off by yourselves.
Explore this out of the way gem.
Well meet again right here for lunch at 2:00.

We two wander off
not too far, no need
to mark our trail with bread crumbs.

We come upon a modest square
anchored by an ancient oak tree
showering shade blessings.

A young man greets us
smiling underneath the oak
guitar in hand.

His smile beckons us to stay.
He pauses, then begins to play
wraps us both

inside his soft ode
to a woman of Malaga
Malaguena

still alluring
enough to send time
on its way without us.

The Troubadour*

I watch you strumming down my street
inside my leafy suburb.

You are not from here
a grizzled troubadour

ponytail and weathered, rutted skin
signs of life lived poorly elsewhere.

You sing about your journey
even as I pass you on my street.

Underneath my notice
comes the leisure of your drawl

Lend a hand my friend . . .
Help me to my next horizon . . .

I keep going for a next appointment
wonder where you're headed.

Next morning there's your music
languid looping through my leafy suburb head

worming deep inside.
I feel the soft and sing song way

you stroll and plead
like someone born to be seductive.

Beige

Beige is comfy, never joins the Light Brigade
rides into the Valley of the Shadow of Death.
To join the brave 600, you must be

Blue to give you hope
Red to urge you on
Green to signal you are winning.

Beige hugs you in your Netflix nights
or while you watch your goldfish
or pass the time inside your eyelids.

Okay as far as these things go
but you don't rise up
take it to the Huns.

I worry that I could be beige.
People who are Blue or Red or Green
embrace, enact, enrage.

Once you think
I might be beige
you are.

WISHES

Facebook Post from the Buddha

It's quite a recognition
a religion named after you.
You'd think more people would be curious
What is The Buddha really like?
He lives a life of contemplation, deprivation.
How come in many pictures he's so fat?

You want to know what it's about?
People come, sit at my feet
offer love gifts
flowers, berries, fruits and nuts
veggies raw and cooked
bread and cakes.

Oh those cakes.
Who am I to turn them down?
People bring a cake, you don't say
No. I don't eat cake.
You're gracious.
I spent years accepting cakes.

And still I made it to Nirvana.

They see the grin.
They want to get here too.
People come to watch me sit
to be here now.
I know there is a lot of me.

If they'd ask about my weight I could explain.
They'd know the real me.
I guess I have to let it go.
Even in Nirvana you still have work to do.
That Dharma Path
full of surprises.

First Girlfriend

Lucky Eddie, just 13
winner of The Susan
the trophy girl friend
in our schoolyard playground
other guys all craved.

The one and only Susan
I somehow got there first.
She sat with me through punchball games
held my hand from time to time.

A body better than my green shoot dreams.
She shared modest bits with me.
Then one day

She vaporized
cast me into limbo

in secret I wept and wondered . . .

Flowered Tumblers 1953*

I am 12. My grownups
fill our stoop in our apartment courtyard
folding chairs and chatter, Sid Caesar and Korea
sodas losing fizz, ice cubes melting in their flowered tumblers.

Inside the spreading summer twilight
my buddy David beckons
we can sneak a peek into a window
maybe catch a woman I saw yesterday.

I follow him down some stairs
up to a ledge below her first floor bedroom.
We climb like spiders
silent clinging to the wall . . .

She's really there
a fleshy jackpot
lying naked on her bed
mirror in her hand.

We watch her watch her self
no thinking why she's doing that
what noise we make
how our gape jaw breathing might just startle her.

It does.
She bolts up shouting.
The husband bursts in roaring
races to our window peeping place.

We flee like antelopes
across the night lawn
back to hide among our herd of grownups
grab some tumblers, sipping slow.

Soon enough the husband races up
where have these kids been
not explaining
why his inquisition.

The herd surrounds us
a grownup male declares
These kids are ours.
They make no trouble.

I look up only half way
blow into the straw
make some quiet bubbles in the soda
in my flowered tumbler

safe inside the lie I'm sure they told for us.

Wanting to Be Dangerous 1955*

I long to join a gang
like West Side Story.
The Sharks, The Jets.
Imagine that for Jewish Kids.
The Herrings gonna get their way tonight . . .
Maria, a boy like that will kiss his mother
He'll be a banker like his brother
stick to your own kind . . .

I beg my dad for days and weeks
let me be in Vito's gang. The Golden Guineas.
At last he gives in.
Alright, but just to keep the books.
Imagine that
Hey Vito, Carmine if you rumble
don't forget, get receipts . . .

I start a secret gang, us Jewish guys.
The Golden Goniffs.
We hang out in the schoolyard
smoke Lucky Stripes
dragging on our chocolate cigarettes
talking tough

Hey, Heshie, lay it on us
tell us about accelerated depreciation.
Sure. First you buy yourself a building.
Are you digging this, mine man?
Heshie, you're the boss
but cheese it, ditch the ciggies
here comes my mom.

We squish them out
chocolate on the soles of our shoes.
The Golden Goniffs.
Mom can never know.

What's Your Favorite Food?

Bacon, bacon, bacon
the devil's temptation
even the righteous

when they smell it
they surrender
to that spoor

curling out from my boyhood
kitchen on Sunday mornings
lifting me

into a trance walk
to my place
at our rosewood kitchen table

where Mom would turn
see me from her stove
black cast iron pan crackling

bubbles popping
three slices forked out
hot and crisp.

I'd watch and drool
like kids do
who expect good news in their future.

Ode to Coney Island

Lawrence Ferlinghetti (1919–2021)

1955, I'm fourteen
Ferlinghetti starts to write
A Coney Island of the Mind.

1957, Uncle Louie takes me to his Coney Island
explains how Nathans' cooks' sweat
gives that special flavor to their fries and dogs.

1958, Ferlinghetti publishes his book.
I buy it, make a special island in my mind
for Ferlinghetti's Coney

where I take Rita Greenberg on a date.
I'm 17, can drive us
in her mother's powder blue Bel-Air

breezing through the summer night
just the two of us, the top down
all the way to Brooklyn.

We park beneath the Wonder Wheel
hop onto the boardwalk holding hands
laugh and gossip on the flow of strangers.

Rita wants to ride the Cyclone.
Urges me, a Cyclone virgin
We'll see all of Coney Island.

I force myself to go.
I stare at Rita's long black shiny hair
blowing in the wind.

Set Fire to the Rain

from Adele

The title of a song I fall for
sung by a woman
her so alluring voice

her song so very pop
so not hip or cool
worms inside my ears.

I hum along, mouth the words
start to dance around our den
allow my dated moves

my desire strong enough to overcome
the wall of doubts about
my remaining sleekness.

The Looks of Love*

In the beginning was our fresh erotic clamor.
Phosphoric flashes exploded through our doubts
blinded and consumed us.
In the mornings we woke hungry
for the wonder in each other's flesh.

Before too long we made those fateful choices
giving up our blood and juices into babies
aliens who conquered spaces we once called our own.
We reveled in their laughter and their triumphs.
The years have helped us blur the endless tending
to their cries and smells and disappointments.

Now our evening mirror shows this older couple
who have kept on all these years
worn smooth like stones in flowing rivers
rounded from the flow of countless days.
We touch each other still
less frequent, more distracted.

We've traveled all these places
fitfully and sometimes self-immersed.
Kept on showing up
because we said we would.
We plan, we laugh, we fight and then repair
worry to each other, to ourselves
choose to still believe there will be ways to love ahead.

Loved One Nostalgia

I found some time for you today
reached out

beyond my elder ruminations
to find you once again

dark and curly hair, peasant blouse
the laughing girl

who long ago conceded
you would go your separate way

that day I claimed
I needed to move on.

I sort through tattered recollections
we were not meant to be

losing touch with you these many years
because I did.

Today I put aside
the pinch of my regrets

make my way back
to our better times.

I'm told you've died.
You cannot hear me now.

Spring Morning on the Back Porch

Chirps, melodies and caws
different nations of birds
separate languages
common hopes

for worms and grubs
who should return, be plentiful
among the twigs and dirt
and in the spring they do.

They creep and crawl
deaf and blind
at ease
inside their modest lives.

I stay here on my porch
avoid the deer ticks,
indifferent parasites
waiting witless for some host

to gorge on
when they can
they will.
Not cruel of them.

Just the way of things.

When I Leave Up the Toilet Seat

My tenured wife points out when I forget
You should put down the toilet seat.

Her critique is true enough
I confess, relent

whisper to myself
how great really is this problem?

What's the harm if she, not me
puts down the seat

covers for me
if you catch my meaning.

When I do show proper form
when she finds the seat is down

she might give voice to her relief
maybe even show some pleasure.

I long for her to catch me
doing something right.

OLD AGE

Still Working After All These Years

I'm getting old,
at least by the numbers
keep time at bay
the stalker.

An acquaintance asks
as if it's the thing to do.
What will you do when you retire?
Waits to hear my cheerful blueprint.

What's the hurry?
I love my work, my colleagues
I'm told I am the best.
I get reassuring compensation.
I'm in good health
according to my growing team of doctors.

Travel to exotic lands?
Play Pickleball or Geezer Golf?
I want another dose of work.
I know how to win
to run the maze
get the cheese at tunnel's end.

But then today
my latest cheese hunt done
I sit behind my desk.
A confession insists.

I could be my oldest colleagues' father
I touch my wrinkled, spotted face.
I think about my slower gait.
They must see these things

whisper to each other.
They think I'm hanging on.
I can't go on
wondering, embarrassed.

I declare *Enough*.
I'll give up all the deadlines and the deference.
I know there'll be gold watches, speeches, *oohs and aahs*.
Then at home, the mornings after . . .

Reflections on a Winter Evening

Some Bad News in Retirement

Canada geese, a flying V
across the indigo winter dusk
syncopated honking cascades
down onto our elders enclave.

Pinched with goose envy
I argue with my landlocked state
the cold lingering, unwelcome
insistent for my attention.

Nothing on the hi-def TV
distracts me
from my struggle
inside frosted windows.

Night air reminders poke me.
Even after gin
no tonic transports me
to reassuring versions of retiring or hereafter.

Now For Some Good News

Morning comes, I do concede
I am still here
the slowly warming sun
moves handsomely across the yard

I own because
I toiled many years
and the bank said
I had what it takes to pay them back.

Much of this because
Mom and Daddy pleasured one hapless end of day
or maybe they had planned it
no matter, my genes and I emerged

and won enough so even I have learned
to stop, watch the late day sunlight
follow cumulus tourists
lollygagging in the sky.

Elder Morning

Less clocks, insistent calls
to hurry up, be somewhere else.
This new morning unfolds without a jump start.
I listen to my chest fill out
strum along inside my head
eyelids gently lift.

I meander inside unconnected musings
allow the urge to raise up
surrender to this portion of my shrinking life.
I lift myself to vertical
creak and laugh it off
park it in the padding of memories.

I linger
reimagine bygone lovers
relish in their pastime succulence.

Across my neatly ordered bedroom
on its proper stand my smartish phone
comfort and umbilicus
plugs me into any world I choose.

Handel or The Beatles on the playlist for today
my life now a Greek diner
lots of choices on the menu
some not fresh
but choose we must.

I pick one for no reason
nothing left to prove
time has come to plug into my ear buds
a duvet of soft encounters.
I've made it to being old.

Mother's Gone*

Your hours have no song or nectar any more
they pass like cats slipping noiseless
outside of your screen door.
Your eyes stare fixed like hazel stones
your world shrunk to food and sleep
perhaps a prize for us, one random day
a word you seem to recognize.

I sit nearby your wheelchair guarding you
from well-wishing friends and strangers
picturing a treeless plain inside your head.
My patter stretches out the moments.

The doctor's words
so easy, clinical, and certain.
Nothing to be done.
She's reached beyond the golden years . . .

I wander back into last May
we sat in plastic chairs.
I praised the Fichus trees around the pool
the cotton shapes drifting in the southern sky.

Not knowing what to do
I reached out to hold your hands
touched your bulging knuckles
caressed the purple roundness of your veins.
You moved your hand, a silent hint
maybe one more frail connection.
Then you drifted off silent as a cloud.

The Wheelchair in the Den

Seventy years since their first date.
Now she sits
hands curled into fists
her eyes stare
down into her lap.

Dad sits across from her.
Unannounced, he pulls himself up
goes over to her, close up, next to her ear
yells *Mildred, Mildred.*
He's probably doing that more, when we're not visiting.

Sometimes she looks at me.
Last week she looked up and shouted "stop yelling at me".
Then she went back.
Yesterday she even held my hand and kissed it.
She asked me to give her a kiss.

He makes sure we know about those trickles.
Brother Mel and I can get away.
Dad's trapped.
He should take care of her.
He's not good at it.

She's run his house
cooked and cleaned for him
paid the bills
invited people over
arranged vacation trips.

Now she's left him here.

Their Suitcase in the Basement

I open the door to the basement
try not to hold the railing
test my balance.
I make it down
flip on the basement lights
look over to the jumble of suitcases

their blue grey Samsonites
the stiff old kind
with handles, but no wheels
from 1980, the year
Dad retired and they finally started
the trips Mom pestered him about
to London, Montreal, Puerto Rico.

I take down the top suitcase.
Their initials, M&J
stamped in crusted latches
I tug on until they open.
Mold aroma from the fabric pockets
rises up into my nose.

Slowly I unwrap
the yellowed newspaper
safeguarding four framed Kodak color photos
Mom, Dad, Brother Mel and me.
One by one
I hold them up.

Mom smiles.
Her hands, arthritis still in hiding
rest on that blue dress
printed with pink roses
I once tried to smell.
Gone 2004.

Dad glows
inside his open collar shirt
one hand on his rod and reel
the other holds aloft for all to see
his trophy dolphin.
Gone 2006.

Mel complies
smile at the camera
a red-haired cherub
freckles cover round and rosy cheeks.
A Gerber baby look alike.
Gone 2020.

I'm the toddler
sitting on the stoop
outside our little stucco house
cuddling a grapefruit
from the tree in our back yard.
Here 2025.

A sting grows inside my eyes
then that dry swallow.
I hold onto each photo
have whispered conversations
then tuck them slowly, gently back
into the suitcase.

August Surrender

A cloudless twilight
full of revelations

lawns dried and patchy
shoulder curvy streets

a soft breeze brings
evening time aromas.

The sun finished with the day
the sky dimmer

trees whisper
lingering goodbyes.

No neighbors out
just us two

refreshed
inside the sunset

look around and at each other
share our hopes in this new home

our new village very planned
55 and over.

All our days are numbered.
Smaller numbers

challenge us to capture peace
nestle in this twilight

let the evening be enough.

The Physics of Time and Me

I've kept a secret wish.
Time would pass me by.
At least slow down for me.
I'd be thought of as a miracle.

It's felt sweet to hold the hope.
No big aches or pains, no paunch.
Yes, some creaking in my joints
a tickle from that tuft of nose hair.

Last week a young man asked
after he had called me *sir.*
Are you really in your eighties?
I smiled. *Thanks for your surprise.*
I feel like I'm still in my 40s.

Then, there really is that nose hair.
And some bad news.
I still can count.

My Plan for Becoming Dead

A sense of humor is common sense dancing
—Clive James

I will pay my respects
to the business of becoming dead
how to dispose of me
leave what's left of me
to those I think deserve it.

I will seek good friends
old people with a sense of humor.
We'll imitate old elephants
gathered 'round each other
to comfort one who's dying.

Better than the elephants
we people know our turn will come
something final
like a dirt nap in forever.
Maybe something better.

Whatever
we old people
those of us who still can laugh
together we will dance.

Resolutions

for my 80s

Sit still on our back porch.
Watch hawks float across the treetops.
Slowly sip my coffee without sugar.

Re-read Baldwin, Camus, Ram Dass.
Highlight ideas I should remember.
Attend that online Ted Talk *Age Is Just a Number.*

Curate playlists: Handel, Lady Gaga, Standup Comics.
Roam through Wikipedia.
Look into Vermeer, Glaciers, The Milky Way.

Make healthy choices.
7,000 steps, 4 times almost every week.
Eat more fruit and fiber.

Savor Madelyne's painting of the Crimson Dahlia.
Watch a TV movie she says might be good.
Rub her feet even when she dozes.

Play iPhone solitaire to help me toward sleep.
Don't worry over bathroom wake up calls .
Sleep or lie in quiet 8 hours, maybe more.

Choose to be an optimist
I'll live through disappointment.
Cry when I'm happy, even if it's public.

Notice when people listen
Not just wait for me to finish.
Say thanks.

Remember
There is nothing left to prove.
I am safe in this moment.

About the Author

Ed Ryterband is a poet, memoirist, standup comic, and psychologist. His poems have been published in *Patterson Literary Review, Two River Times, US1 Worksheets,* and *New Verse News.* He has three collections of poems in print: *Life on Cloud Eight* (Kelsay Books, 2019), *Beyond Cloud Eight* (Kelsay Books, 2020), and *Rain Witness* (Kelsay Books, 2022). *Rain Witness* was nominated in 2022 for a Pushcart Prize. He's publishing a memoir about life under the influence of his immigrant parents called *Who They Were.*

His website is:
edryterband.com

www.ingramcontent.com/pod-product-compliance
Lightning Source LLC
Chambersburg PA
CBHW030910170426
43193CB00009BA/800